HOOPS AND SIGNALS

THE STORY OF A SUSSEX GREAT-GRANDFATHER

JOHN IRELAND

COUNTRY BOOKSS

Published by Country Books/Ashridge Press
Courtyard Cottage, Little Longstone, Bakewell, Derbyshire DE45 1NN
Tel: 01629 640670
e-mail: dickrichardson@country-books.co.uk
www.countrybooks.biz

ISBN 978-1-906789-79-4

British Library Cataloguing in Publication Data.
A catalogue record for this book is available from the British Library.

Printed in Great Britain by 4edge Ltd, Hockley, Essex.

DEDICATION

For
Joshua, Alice, Stan and Kate

CONTENTS

A BROWN PAPER PARCEL

"Those," said Auntie Win, indicating the contents of a brown paper parcel on the top shelf of her bookcase, "those are old, John. They will be yours one day."

Auntie Win was not really my aunt but my father's elderly much loved cousin. In the 1920's she had come with her sister Grace and their widowed mother, Annie Wood, to live in the Sussex village of Balcombe. There they were to look after Annie's bachelor brothers, Tom and Jack after the death of their mother, Ellen Ireland. Ellen's husband Thomas, who had died over twenty years before, is the subject of this story. Auntie Win, as the senior surviving descendant of the Ireland family, was the custodian of the family treasures, many of which had belonged to her grandparents and their parents before them. There was country furniture, for instance, a small round oak stand with an iron clamp on top; this was a holder for a tallow reed lamp, which was in use before wax candles were commonplace and must have been at least two or three centuries old. No-one in Auntie Win's house knew what to do with it, but it had always been there in the corner, and there it remained. And there was a solid oak oval gate-leg table with handmade iron nails sticking out of the surface; Auntie Win would not allow these to be knocked down to make the table more convenient to use "because they're old, you see." There were books, a family bible, and the brown paper parcel.

My mother, who was certainly no hoarder, regarded the brown paper parcel with some misgivings. More rubbish, she thought. After all, Auntie Win was getting on and my mother was wondering who would have the job of clearing the little house when Auntie Win finally left it. Someone was eventually going to have the job of disposing of many things like the brown paper parcel.

She need not have worried. Auntie Win may have been old but she was very well organised. As she prepared to move into pleasant sheltered housing down the road she gave away some of the treasures to carefully selected people, of whom I was a privileged one. There were several photograph albums, for instance, with a hundred or more pictures of friends and relatives. Sadly Auntie Win's eyesight was getting very poor, and she was unable to tell who was in many of the photographs, although a bit of detective work has enabled one or two to be identified and

"Aunty Win" 1962

included in this story. She arranged for other treasures to be sold, albeit for a song (although she had been right about the nails in the gate-leg table, whose "original condition" was praised by the auctioneer). The brown paper parcel was given to my mother with instructions that it be handed on to me. "Here you are," said my mother, flicking the dust away. "You'd better have a look inside before you throw it out." So I did, but there was no question of throwing it away.

The parcel contained twenty-odd pocket notebooks, all filled with the handwriting of Thomas Ireland, my great-grandfather. Three books had columns of figures, with words whose meaning would have to await understanding of their context, like "short pink", "fourteens" and "bottle". The other books were mainly Thomas's diaries, covering most of the years between the early 1860's and the 1890's. Subsequently another of the diaries, that for 1884, turned up in the West Sussex Records Office at Chichester, having been bought by them from a bookseller in Romsey. How it came to him is anyone's guess. The diary writings in all the books were interspersed with newspaper cuttings, gardening tips, recipes or other notes made by Thomas on whatever caught his eye.

I read on. At times it made difficult reading because although the handwriting was carefully formed it was sometimes indistinct and many of the names and places mentioned were unfamiliar to me. Gradually however the picture emerged of the life and work of a Victorian Sussex countryman and through him a record of the doings of the village in which he lived. At one level the collection is certainly not a literary masterpiece, indeed much of the content is quite humdrum. But, considered as the work of a largely self-taught artisan to whom people in the village would come for help with reading and writing their letters, and as a detailed account of how this man spent at least the second half of his life, it forms a remarkable document. Auntie Win and perhaps my father had known their grandfather quite well. They would have had plenty to tell about him that would have fleshed out his story. But they are now long gone and have taken their memories with them. And yet the diaries of Thomas reveal so much about the man that I feel I know him as well as if he were sitting here beside me now.

One of my earliest memories is as a three year-old spending the first few bomb-threatened weeks of World War II with my mother in the cottage of Balcombe waterworks, up in the woods a couple of miles outside the village on the Handcross road. My great-uncle Jack (another John Ireland) was the manager here, where he lived with his brother Tom, and where the two uncles were looked after by their unmarried nieces, "Auntie Win" and "Auntie Grace". How we all squeezed into the little cottage I can't remember, but after six weeks or so of the "phoney war" my mother took me back to the outer London suburbs, where ironically the blitz was to start a few months later.

Subsequently down the years there were many visits to Balcombe, both to the waterworks and later when the four moved down into the village. Then, in about 1960 with retirement in view, my parents had a bungalow built in Brett's Orchard, which was then my home for the next two or three years. Coincidentally this was right next door to Diamond Cottage, where my father's grandparents, Thomas and Ellen Ireland, had lived for many years.

So in one way or another I have known Balcombe all my life, and have always regarded it as a sort of spiritual home. When I started to read my great-grandfather's diaries, nothing seemed more natural than that I should try to find out more about him, his life, work and family, and through him about the village where he spent his whole life. In this way the process began which eventually ended up as this little book.

So here, with heartfelt gratitude to my great-grandmother Ellen, to her daughter Annie and to Auntie Win who between them faithfully kept the brown paper parcel for over seventy years (without apparently ever reading what was in it), and to my mother who did not throw it out either, but who all treasured it and its contents eventually to hand it on to me, is the story, much of it told by himself, of my great grandfather, Thomas Ireland.

JFI
Autumn 2012

What was in the brown paper parcel

CHAPTER 1

WOODLAND AND RAILWAY

Thomas Ireland's life began, continued and ended in the village of Balcombe, surrounded by the low wooded hills of the mid-Sussex weald. The nearest towns are Crawley, now a busy adjunct to Gatwick airport but then little more than a village, and Haywards Heath, today a prosperous commuter town on the main London to Brighton railway line, which until the railway came was an insignificant hamlet. Thomas was born in Balcombe on 14th December 1824, when England was still largely an agricultural land, and died there on 5th January 1898, by which time the economy of the country was powered by the heavy industry of the Midlands and the North. In some ways Thomas's life remained untouched by these profound movements, but because of them the second half of his life was rather different from the first.

What changed Thomas's life was the coming of the railway in the 1840's. As a boy he would have been aware of the changes that were afoot elsewhere. He would have watched the grand carriages rattling along the turnpike through Balcombe to take their wealthy owners to the increasingly popular watering place of Brighton. In the 1830's he would doubtless have heard tell of the new railways in the North, some of which, like that between Liverpool and Manchester, no longer carried just coal and other goods, but were now taking passengers, who until then had travelled only by coach. From fellow villagers he may even have heard that a group of businessmen had in mind that the London to Brighton route might offer a profitable opportunity for such a railway development. He would have picked up local speculation about possible routes for the railway, and of the impact it might have on his village and its surroundings.

Until then he had worked in the woodland industry alongside his father, uncles and brothers, as many of his other relatives and ancestors had done before him. They were engaged in the manufacture of barrel hoops, of which more later. This was essentially a rural craft industry, involving little contact with people outside the village other than the carters and bargemen who took the hoops to the coopers in nearby towns to make the barrels that were the equivalent of the packing cases of a later age. The railways changed all that. There had been a great influx of workers into Balcombe in the late 1830's and early 1840's when the London to Brighton railway was constructed (the viaduct and the tunnel at Balcombe were major civil engineering projects involving a huge labour force). Although these workers left the area when their work was completed their presence for two or three years in the hitherto remote little village must have made locals much more aware of the world outside. But the real change came when the railway opened in 1841. Then it became quick, easy and relatively cheap to send the hoops by rail much farther afield to where maybe they could command a better price, although they were also exposed to more competition. More significantly, as communications improved so greatly it became possible for people to move about much more easily.

All these factors came together for Thomas to give his life a new direction. The market for wooden barrel hoops was over the long term potentially in decline. This may have been because of increased competition, or perhaps coopers and others were turning to iron hoops instead of wooden ones. So although there would be work for the hoop-makers and other woodland industry workers for another fifty or sixty years the burgeoning industrial economy, including the coming of the railways, meant that ultimately there would be no more need for them. In fact hoop making continued to decline until the first World War, and by the 1920's it had died out almost completely. Perhaps because he saw the signs of a potential downturn in his trade, perhaps because he had higher aspirations, or perhaps because he simply wanted more money than hoop making could provide, Thomas decided to find additional employment. So it was that in 1852 he joined the London and Brighton & South Coast Railway Company, eventually becoming a signalman. He continued to make barrel hoops, though, but in his diaries he carefully distinguishes between his "work" in the woods and his "duty" in the signal box. The diaries show that he seemed to be equally busy in both these very different occupations, at least until he retired from the railway in 1893.

Several routes for the new railway were considered by the London & Brighton Railway Company ("& South Coast" was added later). Advised by Robert Stephenson, the by now famous railway engineer. John Rennie favoured the most direct route and George Bidder suggested one that avoided sharp bends and steep gradients. Stephenson himself preferred Bidder's route, but commercial considerations won the day:- "The [Bidder] route is six miles longer than the direct route. Taking two pence to be the average charge per mile to the traveller, this will impose on him a shilling extra charge." So thought the Company, which therefore chose Rennie's route, and in July 1837 this was the one that duly received Parliament's permission.

There were still hills and valleys to be crossed, though, and the route involved the construction of four tunnels, at Merstham, Balcombe, Haywards Heath and Clayton Hill, plus a viaduct across the River Ouse just south of Balcombe. This viaduct was completed in 1841 and is one of the most elegant examples of early railway architecture in England. "*The London to Brighton line,*" records Thomas in a note at the end of his 1889 diary, "*opened to Haywards Heath on July 12th 1841 and thence to Brighton in September the same year.*" The whole project had cost over £2½ million and had employed some 6,000 men, of whom several hundred had lived around Balcombe, probably in special encampments.

The line passes about half a mile to the west of the village, and the massive works of Balcombe tunnel and the viaduct are only a mile or two north and south respectively. Construction traffic would have

Balcombe viaduct, from a postcard of 1905

churned up the narrow muddy lanes, and the disturbance to the little community must have been considerable.

However, once the railway was in service it must have transformed the lives of Balcombe people. Before the coming of the railway it would have taken a long day to get to Brighton on foot. London was accessible only by stage-coach, unless you were well-off enough to have your own horse and carriage, and even then the journey would have taken you at least half a day. By train you could now reach Brighton within the hour and London in a couple of hours or so. Moreover it was reasonably cheap. You could get to London for six shillings and sixpence (32½p) and Brighton for half-a-crown (12½p). The horizons of Thomas and the other villagers suddenly widened, and their lifestyle, confined almost entirely to Balcombe and its surroundings, gave way almost overnight to a more complex, sophisticated, and perhaps a more enjoyable one.

These changes must have had a profound effect on young Thomas, although what he actually thought of it he didn't say, or a least he didn't write it down. What we do know is that in October 1852 the 28 year-old was taken into the employment of the London Brighton &

South Coast Railway as a "tunnelman" with wages of nineteen shillings (95p) per week. In those early days it was felt that passengers in the open-top carriages might become alarmed at being plunged into the darkness of railway tunnels. So the tunnels were lined with white-washed corrugated iron and lit at intervals by gas jets. The fuel for these jets came from specially constructed gas plants at the entrance to each tunnel, and the duties of a tunnelman presumably included tending this device. Before long smoke from the locomotives dirtied the white paint and draught from passing trains blew the jets out, so the practice was discontinued. But the designation of tunnelman was retained, and so Thomas remained for years.

Eventually, in May 1875, Thomas was officially made a "signalman", earning a rise to one guinea (£1.05) a week. Railway signalling had come a long way. At first its sole function was to prevent tail-end collisions in tunnels, so it was sufficient for someone, often the local policeman, simply to wave an engine driver on if it was safe to proceed. Later this task passed to the tunnelmen, who were housed in small cabins and equipped with telegraphs to inform them when the tunnel was clear and so safe to receive the next train. This was an altogether higher level of responsibility, leading to the new title and higher wages, and eventually led to the development of modern block signalling.

Thomas spent most of his railway employment at the "North End", which was by now the signal box at the end of the tunnel farthest from the village. Auntie Win said that at one point he was offered a promotion, by which he would have become Station Master at Balcombe, but that would have involved living in the Station House on the station itself, and he felt that such a move would not be safe for the young family he had by then acquired. Although Thomas remained at heart a true countryman with his roots in the rural economy and way of life of the village, yet his duties with the technologically developing railway system and his dealings with officials of the railway company were of a quite different order. In a way this rural Victorian became a harbinger of the 20th century. And it was all down to the railway.

By the time of this 1905 postcard the "North End" signal box had been removed.

By the time of this 1905 postcard the "North End" signal box had been removed

CHAPTER 2

HOOPS FROM COPPICE

A untie Win always spoke of her grandfather as a railwayman, a
signalman on the London to Brighton line. And so he was, at
least from 1852 until he retired from the railway company in the
1890's.

But Thomas would have thought of himself primarily as an artisan,
a practitioner of the trade at which he and his father, brothers and
uncles had worked all their lives, and at which Thomas himself was
active right into his old age. That was the trade of the maker of
barrel hoops, bands usually of hazel or ash that bound together the
staves of so-called "slack" barrels.

Barrels were of two basic sorts. One kind, the wet barrel, was used
for the transport and storage of liquids, beer and wine, for example.
These were mostly re-used over and over again during their life. They
consisted of shaped staves held together by iron bands, and were
tapered towards the top and bottom to ensure that when the staves
were forced together by the bands the joints between them were as
tight as possible. With use the wooden staves swelled as the liquid
soaked into them and so the barrel became even more watertight. The
bulbous shape of the barrel had the added advantage of making it
easier to manoeuvre when it was rolled along the ground.

The other sort of barrel was the slack barrel, which was used for
dry goods, anything from nails, cement or gunpowder to fruit,
vegetables or tobacco. For the most part slack or dry barrels did not
have to be completely watertight, and as the staves did not have to be

so tightly forced together were less
bulbous in shape. These barrels were
bound with wooden hoops, such as those
made by Thomas. When the barrels
reached their destination they were
emptied and the hoops cut away to be
used as firewood. The staves of the
dismantled barrel were bundled up and
sent back as 19th century flat-packs to be
re-assembled and used all over again. So
at least as long as slack barrels were in
use there was a constant requirement for
barrel hoops, and Thomas could be sure
of a continuing demand for his wares.

A slack barrel

Barrel hoop making was one of a large
number of what were known as the underwood trades. These
depended on the practice of coppicing, which has been carried on for
hundreds if not thousands of years. Trees are cut down almost to
ground level. The stumps, or "stools", are encouraged to send up
shoots which become straight poles. These are cut down every ten or
fifteen years, leaving the stools to send up more shoots, and so the
cycle starts all over again. If maintained the process ensures a
constantly renewable source of material and sometimes the coppice
stools are many hundreds of years old.

Coppice wood has been used for many purposes. At one time it
was used mainly as a source of firewood, but the presence of iron ore
in areas such as in Sussex, Surrey and Hampshire, where there were
also extensive woodlands, led to its use to make charcoal to smelt the
ore there. Now only the names of the many "hammer woods" or
"forge woods" remain in the Weald to remind us of this industry. But
in the 18th and 19th centuries coal mining in Wales, the Midlands and
the North proved a much more efficient fuel and so the ore was
processed there, leaving little need for charcoal for this purpose.
However, coppice wood has always been used for traditional rural
items such as broom handles, rakes, hurdles, thatching rods, hop
poles and of course barrel hoops. And with the industrialisation that

Charcoal burners, Balcombe Forest

followed the Napoleonic wars there came increased demand for manufactured goods like pit props, scaffolding, bobbins for the textile industry, clogs, toys, tanning bark and many others. So coppice wood found new outlets. Barrel hoops, too, had been made for many hundreds of years, and so, despite the long-term decline in the trade, during the mid-19th century the burgeoning economy made ever-increasing demands on the supply of these commodities.

Owners of woodland suitable for coppice would sell areas of standing trees at annual sales held each autumn and probably conducted by auction. Thomas's diaries show that he regularly attended these sales, but although he sometimes recorded what prices were paid, he did not usually buy the wood himself. He did write on one occasion on 4th December 1868: *I went to the Wood Sale at Pound Hill and bid for the Street Wood £8 and £8/5/- but did not have it.* But as a rule he probably went along just to keep an eye on things so as to know what the going rate was. The usual purchasers were wood dealers, middlemen who had some capital behind them and who understood the value the coppice would yield once processed, and hence their potential profit. Once the woods were sold wood cutters moved in to fell the coppice. The wood dealer then arranged for the coppiced poles to be sorted by thickness and length according to the type of product they were to be used for. Then it was the turn of the underwood tradesmen, the men who specialised in the various products, such as the hoop makers.

The hoop makers would select the coppice that suited them and "set out" the poles according to the different sizes of hoop. These could vary considerably, from four foot long "bottle" which was used for the small water casks carried by workmen through the six-foot "firkin" and the 9'7" "hogshead" to the "fourteen footers" for heavy sugar barrels. Each pole was fitted into a device known as a brake and split ("cleft") into three or four or more lengths, using a sort of single-handled draw-knife called a fromard or froe, carefully tapped along the grain. The more skilled the worker the more lengths he could get out of a pole. Next the

A Sussex hoop maker splitting rods on a brake

strips were clamped to a "horse" (Thomas used a variant of this which he called his France board) and shaved to the right thickness with a two-handled draw-knife, taking great care to leave the bark on the outside and not to chip out any knots. Usually the strips were coiled on a special frame, but Thomas seems to have passed them on unbent. The finished hoops were bundled together, typically thirty or so at a time, although sometimes as many as sixty, for onward transport. This was arranged by the wood dealer. He would previously have negotiated how much he would pay the wood cutters and the other tradesmen like Thomas. Thomas, having attended the wood sale and ascertained the price paid for the woods, no doubt had an idea of what he could expect to receive.

The wood dealer would also know where and how he could get the best price for the finished products. If he knew what he was doing he could well become a rich man, buying himself a horse and cart and perhaps his own land. Thomas's Uncle John (yet another John Ireland) was such a man. From humble beginnings he became his own master, with a fine house on the London road out of Balcombe as well as other properties in the area, and Thomas records that in 1805 he was a founder member of the (businessmen's) club at the Bell Inn in Horley.

Thomas left careful accounts of how his part of the system worked. Thomas himself was the oldest and was the leader of the small team of his brothers, John, three years his junior, George, six years younger, and "the boys" Jonathan and James, respectively eleven and sixteen years younger. Sometimes others joined them, but although the men evidently worked together Thomas always indicated the total number of hoop bundles made by each man and thus each individual's earnings. Thomas's team would undertake to produce barrel hoops from the coppice-wood in a particular piece of woodland. He noted down the number of bundles of hoops produced by each man, priced each bundle according to the length and nature of the hoops contained in it, then totalled the amount earned by each individual. This formed the basis of the account presented to the dealer. Wagonloads of bundles of hoops would then be taken to the coopers or barrel-makers.

Until now it has been believed that hoop-making only took place shortly after the wood was coppiced. By convention the season began at Michaelmas (29th September) and ended by Lady Day (25th March), but according to Thomas's records it sometimes went on into June or July, using up coppice that had been cut some time previously. The men were then generally absorbed into agricultural or bricklaying work until the next season. So, for example, James is reported as having worked as a bricklayer in November 1862, September 1878 and May 1884, while John worked on the college, by which Thomas no doubt meant Ardingly College that was under construction three or four miles away. Although Thomas and his group sometimes worked on into the summer, hoop making seldom appears as an official occupation because the censuses were taken every ten years in April, when the hoop makers were generally otherwise employed. The brothers were shown on the census returns as labourers, while Thomas himself appeared as a railway employee, and his diaries show that he worked on the railway throughout the year, evidently relying on his "duty" as a signalman for his income during the summer months.

For his part of the story Thomas's records are meticulous as far as they go, but they do not cover every year and there is some information he does not give us. The income of the hoop makers seems to have been quite variable and not always dependent on how much work they did. The price Thomas got for his larger hoops was much higher than for the small ones, although the amount of work was probably much the same. So in 1847 fourteen and fifteen footers both fetched 1/1d per bundle, whereas kilderkin was worth only 5¾d and the chips used for bakers' ovens brought in a mere 1d. In 1869-70 he records earnings of 13/7 d for 27 bundles of hoops made in Hagland Wood, whereas in Mill Lane that year he got only 8/4d for 26 bundles, but he doesn't say which hoops the bundles consisted of. The price paid at the autumn sales by the wood dealers probably reflected the value of the yield, so maybe the "better" woods could produce larger and better value hoops. So for example at the 1868 sale in Pound Hill Mr Webber paid £3/15/- per acre for Syron Wood. Thomas made 107 bundles of hoops there that year, earning £2/1/1d, or just over 4½d per bundle. But for Beachams Wood the same Mr Webber paid £9/10/- per acre and Thomas made 437 bundles for £19/6/8d - about 11d each. Thomas doesn't say how the woods were allocated to the different groups of tradesmen, but he would have known from his own local knowledge and from attending the sales which ones could be worked to the best advantage.

His income over the six- or eight-month season seems to have fluctuated. In 1849 it was about £63, which appears to have been earned by Thomas himself. In 1868-69 his earnings from hoop making were down to £34/4/11½d, but this must be seen against the fact that by then he was also employed on the railway and so had much less time for his "work" in the woods. It was hard work, though. At the end of the first week in June 1874 Thomas found time to write on the Sunday evening:

At station all day and all the week since Monday morning – and from Monday morning till tonight. I worked about 105 or 106 hours in Sarels Shaw morning and night all but last night and had my tea at home last Monday evening and not a meal at home till tonight

In 1860 the average per capita income in Britain was 12/4d per week. In 1867 even farm labourers, amongst the lowest paid workers in the country, could command 14/- per week. Thomas's income was evidently better than this for the most part, although from his records it emerges that hoop-making provided a rather erratic wage, and it must have been a bit risky to rely on it to keep a growing family. Small wonder that Thomas's brothers relied on casual work during the four months or so before the woods were sold off and coppiced to make available the material for hoop-making, while Thomas himself turned to working for the railway company to augment his income.

At any rate it looks as if in keeping down two jobs Thomas had plenty of energy. That does not mean that he had no time or energy for other matters.

A "froe" or "fromard"

CHAPTER 3

CHURCH AND CHAPEL

In the 19th century England was a nation of great public and private piety. In the public sphere there was a good deal of building of churches, both on the Catholic wing of the Oxford Movement with its dreamy, idealized gothic churches and on the Protestant wing with its thousands of small non-conformist chapels that sprang up throughout the land. At the private level, too, religion played an important part. Fortunately so from the point of view of the family researcher, because the main events in people's lives were conducted as a matter of course through the church. Baptism, marriage, burial – all were faithfully recorded in parish or other ecclesiastical records.

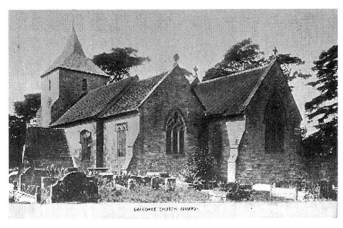

St Mary's Parish Church, Balcombe

So we know that Thomas Ireland was baptized as an infant into the Church of England on 3rd April 1825, that he was married on 26th November 1862, also by the Church of England, and that he was buried in February 1898 in the Anglican churchyard of Balcombe (see Appendix 2 burial J21). As with most people of his day, the key events in his life took place in the context of the established church of the land. Moreover, he clearly attended the church himself, at least from time to time. His diaries tell of his children being christened there and his wife being "churched" after childbirth. He also records when he, various relatives and other villagers had the banns read before their wedding. So perhaps he was a more regular attender than the diaries otherwise appear to give him credit for.

But the diaries show that he had another religious loyalty, too. In his diaries for the years from 1861 to 1874 (except for those for 1864 and 1865, which are missing) Thomas records on no fewer than 130 occasions the biblical text for the sermons preached at the little wooden clapboard building, known as Providence Chapel, beside the railway bridge in Rocky Lane, Balcombe. That certainly indicates more than a passing interest in the religious approach of this little Strict Baptist community. We cannot tell whether he attended the chapel before 1861, which is more or less when the diaries begin, or after 1874, when references to it cease. But over that period he was clearly what was known in those days as "a consistent hearer". According to the Strict Baptist Historical Society this chapel has a tale to tell.

"Used at first as a shop and for many years as a chapel [*the building*] has an interesting story. It was purchased in 1858 by Joseph Worsley, but the

story commences some twelve or thirteen years earlier. About the years 1845-1846 week[*day*] evening services were held in the house of Mrs Gammon by Edward Arnold, pastor of the Strict Baptist Chapel at Cuckfield, but such was the local enmity against the preaching of the Gospel that the whole village rose up in protest. Given the opprobrious name of "water dogs", the Baptists were bawled at and maligned, persecuted and oppressed, until so outrageous became the opposition that the services were given up. But not for long; Mr Arnold, after six years' ministry at Cuckfield, felt encouraged to make a fresh attempt at Balcombe. A Strict Baptist Church was formed on October 26th 1851 by Mr Cooper of Crab Tree, and a chapel was erected and opened by Mr Sedgwick of Brighton. Just exactly what happened to this cause it is difficult to say, but before 1854 the chapel had been converted into cottages and services were being held in the house of a Mrs Streeter. Among the ministers who came to preach during this period was Joseph Worsley of Brighton who in 1858 provided the second chapel, which was opened in August of that year. Soon it was filled to overflowing, and a good congregation gathered for many years. But the chapel or the site on which it was built was private property and in 1874 this was the cause of much trouble. In later years oversight of the cause was undertaken by various local ministers."

It is worth noting that 1874, the year of "much trouble", is also the last year in which Thomas records the names of the preachers at the chapel.

The chapel celebrated its Jubilee in 1908 but seems not to have survived beyond World War I. None of this history is reported by Thomas, whose references to the chapel are confined almost entirely

Providence Chapel, Balcombe

to a note of the preacher's name and the text on which he preached. One wonders what use Thomas made of this information. The answer is probably none at all; he just liked recording facts for their own sake.

The late Dr Kenneth Dix of the Strict Baptist Historical Society observed that membership and other records of the little chapel have evidently not survived, but that in any case Thomas would not have been a member of it, or he would not have had his children christened in the parish church. However, in common with many Victorians he clearly enjoyed listening to sermons. Dr Dix commented that:-

"Many of the texts preached from were taken from the Old Testament prophets. These books, together with the Book of Psalms, were favourites. The method of the preachers was to spiritualise the verse chosen in terms of New Testament teaching. In these sermons there was an emphasis on sin and human depravity...of being brought to a sense of guiltiness before God, and then finding mercy in Christ. The texts chosen by the preachers at Balcombe more than suggest that this type of preaching would have been almost the sole diet for these people, as indeed it was (and still is in some places) in many similar chapels in Sussex and elsewhere. Only rarely were these verses dealt with in the context of the book in which they were found, and only rarely were practical matters dealt with. Sadly, one diet for every meal!"

Thomas must have known his Bible well. To judge by the number of occasions on which he bought a new bible or "(New) Testament" he must have simply worn them out by constant use, probably carrying one all the time in his pocket. One of his bibles has the dates of the events it describes printed in the margin. It says that the creation as described in Genesis 1:1 occurred in the year 4004 B.C. That date was widely accepted by biblical scholars who based it on Old Testament genealogies. It would certainly have been favoured by such authorities as *"The Rock"* and *"The Earthen Vessel"*, the religious periodicals so much loved by Thomas, who frequently quoted them as authoritative. This copy of the Bible was inscribed inside the cover with the date 1863 when Thomas acquired it. Now, in 1859, just four years before that, Charles Darwin had published his "Origin of Species" with its evidence for the evolution of the natural world proving that the earth had been in existence for many millions of years, thus refuting the date of 4004 B.C. The upset this caused amongst the conservative Christian establishment was enormous. Furious argument ensued in the press, which must have included the evangelical publications read by Thomas. It is inconceivable that he did not know about it, and highly likely that he would have held very strong anti-evolutionary views. Yet nowhere in the diaries does this controversy get even a mention. It is as if he simply ignored it. Maybe the enormity of the new thinking was simply too much for him to take in, or perhaps he thought it was simply a cranky modern fad that would soon be forgotten.

Thomas's reading was not confined to the Scriptures, or even to matters of religion. The diaries are peppered with extracts from newspapers, sometimes cut out and pasted in, usually inside the cover of one of the notebooks, or sometimes hand written and quoted verbatim (*see* Appendix 1). But many of the extracts show the real passion of his religious views – anti-popery. He was vehement in his condemnation of the Church of Rome and all its works, scouring the papers and periodicals for anything that would back his prejudices. The following extracts were all written out by hand. They give something of the flavour.

"The Reforming Princes of Germany drew up a formal protest or declaration of their opinions in which they appealed from the Diet of Worms to the Word of God, and from the emperor Charles to Jesus Christ. This protest they read before the Diet. From that day the name Protestant has been given to all those who hold the truth in opposition to the Church of Rome." (Follows the 1891-1895 diary. Probably copied or paraphrased from an article in a nonconformist journal like "*The Earthen Vessel*")

"At the present day, when Ritualistic lecturers such as Dr. Lee are preaching a reunion with Rome on the altered grounds that it is 'to Rome we owe our Christianity', the able volume before us comes to us most welcome. It is the very ablest refutation we have yet seen of the insolent assumptions of St. Augustine and the Romish Church, as the founders of early British Christianity..." (From the back of the 1869 diary, this newspaper cutting reviews a newly published book, *Perambulator*, or the *Lost Church Found* by Rev. C.T. Collins Trelawney)

"Popery is a poison that taints everything it touches." (1868 notebook p.18)

"Adam Smith has correctly said – 'The Church of Rome is the most formidable combination that ever was formed against the authority and security of civil government, as well as against the liberty, reason and happiness of mankind.'"
(Ibid p.23)

"Mr Verity, at Mr Murphy's lecture at Manchester, said he had only one remedy for Ireland, and that was the one adopted by Cromwell, who quieted Irish disaffection in a week. Cromwell went over to Ireland, dealt vigorously with the Romish Priest and no more was heard of disaffection." (Ibid p.26. This is the most extreme example of Thomas's prejudice. One wonders what he would have made of 20th century Irish history.)

"Sin lies very light upon the conscience when its burden can be taken away by confession to a priest and its guilt washed away by absolution and penance." (Ibid. p.42. Here lies the core of Thomas's ideas on sin and guilt. See Kenneth Dix's comments above.)

"The religious liberty which all Her Majesty's subjects happily enjoy is owing to the Christian Church in this Country *having accepted the principals (sic) of the reformation and recognized the supremacy of the Sovereign as the representative of the State, not only in matters temporal but in matters ecclesiastical. This is the stronghold of our spiritual freedom. So long as there is in this country the connection, through the medium of a Protestant Sovereign between the State and the Protestant Church religious liberty is secure. B. Disraeli"* (Ibid p.12. For Thomas religion was a public as well as a private matter.)

The Church of England has always been a "broad church", comprising both catholics and evangelicals and all those in between. Thomas presumably felt its catholic element was too strong and that was why he partly defected to the little Baptist chapel, although he seems to have left it, perhaps because of the "much trouble" of 1874, or maybe he simply got fed up with its negative approach. At any rate, the version of the faith served up there was evidently a pretty cheerless affair, based on the view that we are all wicked and need saving from our own depravity. Thomas himself, it should be said, does not give the impression of being particularly guilt-ridden. Indeed, he appears well-balanced and at ease with himself. Although in his view it is the Church of Rome that bears the real responsibility for the world's ills, the extreme Protestant alternative that he espoused for a time was itself very grim and unattractive.

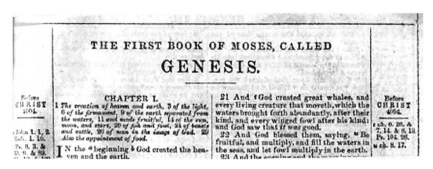

From Thomas's bible. The date of the creation of the world is given as 4004 BC.

CHAPTER 4

MAKING ENDS MEET

Thomas was never well off. But he was never poor, and by the standards of his day he lived quite comfortably. True, considered as a railway signalman he did not earn much. In 1867, according to Baxter's National Income, quoted by Geoffrey Best in *Mid-Victorian Britain 1851-1875*, the average weekly wage of a railway worker was within the range of 21/- to 23/- or £1.05 to £1.15. At that time Thomas was earning 19/- (95p) a week, although he was "raised", as he put it, to 21/- in 1875 and again to 22/- (£1.10) in 1884. Then in 1893 he was superannuated on £17/3/4d per annum, a mere 6/6d (32p) a week.

But while he no doubt regarded his wages from the railway company as a steady income that he could count on he probably thought of himself all along primarily as what he had been brought up to be, a barrel hoop maker. Chapter 2 shows that he could sometimes get quite a good income from this source, but that he couldn't count on it. In 1867-68 the group of Thomas and his brothers earned about 2/11d per man per day over the six-month season, but the next year it was down to 1/9¾d. And in 1869-70, when Thomas was working on his own for some reason and was probably fitting in his "work" with his "duties" in the signal box, he earned only 7½d a day. The brothers seemed to have earned more than Thomas did, but he was constrained by his railway duty schedule and could not spend as much time hoop making as they did.

In view of this, when looking at how Thomas managed his

financial affairs let us set his income from hoop making to one side, and assume that he was relying solely on his railway wages. We can factor in his hoop making income later. On that basis his weekly income in the mid-1860's was of the order of £1 a week. On that he was keeping himself and his wife and two children (five more were to come). His rent amounted to 3/- a week (from 1882 it was 4/-) so he had about 17/- (85p) for his family to live on. Not a fortune, one might think.

But it was not quite as stark as that. Thomas and Ellen probably never bought much food. Their vegetables were grown in their own garden (*see* Appendix 1), or else in the ones Thomas kept beside his signal box by the tunnel or at the station. Thomas had to pay rent for these, though. On 16th June 1870 he records rather grudgingly:

Rent for ground at station for garden stopped out of this fortnight's pay, viz. 1/6d (7½p).

And they almost never bought meat. Chickens and the resultant eggs would have come from the garden, and like many country people they kept a pig. The animal was bought at about ten weeks of age and killed at between six and twelve months. Thomas, of course, helpfully kept records of all this, and it is worth setting down in full his account of 3rd February 1866:

Killed the pig in the morning. We had him September 9. He eat about 12 bushels (= 96 gallons) of Sharps at 2/- per bushel and ½ bushel of whole peas at 2/7½d and about a gallon of ground peas at 5½d per bushel and about 3 bushels of acorns, which is about £1/10/3d. Gave for him £1. He cost about £2/10/3d. He weighed about 16 stone 2 lbs hot, say 16 stone cold which is 3/1½d per stone (i.e. about 2¾d or1p per pound). Mother salted it down at night.

On this basis, if a family of four or five ate four pounds of meat in a week it would have cost about 11d. Sometimes the pig meat was smoked: *Hung the meat up Wm Marchant's chimney,* writes Thomas on 30th October, 1866. And on 21st April 1869 *Robert Henly hung our meat up his chimney*. Evidently Mr Marchant and Mr Henly burned only wood on their fires, whereas Thomas the railwayman may have used some coal on his, which of course would have made it unsuitable for smoking food. At any rate, it appears that the smoking took about a month, for on 27th November: *Took the bacon from Wm Marchant's*.

Thomas's family acquired meat from other sources, too, through gift or barter. So on 16th December 1868: *Mother cooked hare I had given me*, and on 25th November 1869: *Had a hare of Mr Hankey – given me last night the 24th*. December 1868 seems to have been a fortunate month for the Irelands, for on Sunday 13th: *We all had dinner at Mother's. Roast goose of Jonathan's*.

In the late summer and autumn the family would go nutting, gleaning hazel nuts from the woods. On one occasion they gathered 1½ gallons of nuts shelled. No doubt this supplemented their own diet, but perhaps they sold them as well. They also gathered acorns for the pig, sometimes gathering up to nine gallons of them in 2½ hours. And after the grain harvest they went gleaning, or "leasing", as Thomas called it. This word seems to be derived from "leaze" (compare French "laisser"), an unused or abandoned field. Corn was still often cut by hand in the nineteenth century. This was an inefficient process compared with that of a modern harvester, and plenty of grain was scattered on the ground. Having taken his harvest the farmer would permit enterprising folk who did not object to back-breaking hard work to follow the reapers into the fields to gather the ears for themselves. According to Thomas the grain would then be taken to the local mill to be threshed and ground into flour. A lot of hard work, but it all helped.

Flour was an important and staple food and you could not rely for your whole supply on a few days leasing, so you had to buy it from the miller. On Tuesday, 5th August, 1862 Thomas says he paid 9/2d for 1 bushel, or about 48 lbs. A few weeks later, on 10th September, he paid 4/4d for ½ bushel. At that time, before his marriage, he was living with this mother and brothers, who probably ate large quantities of bread. A family of four or five could easily get through a two-pound loaf a day, and perhaps more. So Thomas's 1½ bushels of flour may have lasted the family a month at most, assuming it was used for baking both bread and pastry, and would have cost 13/6d (67p), or about 3/6½d a week.

There is a curious occurrence over a week in June 1878.

Tom (the second of Thomas's sons) *begun Alder Flawing ... near the Tunnel.*

It would appear that this meant stripping the bark off the coppiced alder rods. Then Thomas records that

I was tying up alder rinds.

But a day or two before that

...we got some Rinds tonight that I bought last Saturday and paid ...4/- for them.

The bark of the alder contains the anti-inflammatory salicin and as a decoction it has various soothing medicinal applications, for instance as a wash for sore eyes and to relieve itching. Perhaps Thomas used it for his own family, or perhaps he was able to sell it to a pharmacist. But why he should also have bought the rinds, quite expensively, is a mystery

Thomas gives little information on the cost of other foods and materials, but an article entitled "Life on a Guinea a Week" from "The Nineteenth Century (1888)" on the "Victorian Web" site suggests average costs (presumably for a family, although it does not say so) of a range of goods and services at the time and may serve to flesh out the rather sketchy picture Thomas gives us. With this addition and on Thomas's information his weekly budget could have looked something like the following. Costs taken from the "Victorian Web" are marked with an asterisk*.

Income

Railway Company wages	£-/19/-
Hoop making	
(see below)	
	£-/19/-

Expenditure

Rent	£-/3/-
Meat	£-/-/11d
Flour	£-/3/6d *
Butter, milk, tea, sugar	£-/4/- *
Paraffin, candles, soap	£ -/-/10d *
	£-/12/3½d

Which leaves £-/6/8½d. for all other expenses. According to the "Victorian Web" these could have included:-

Boots for the family	£-/1/8d *
Clothes for the family	£-/3/-*
School fees	£-/-/4d *
	£-/5/-

Total expenditure for the week could therefore have been £-/17/3½d

Some of the figures based on the diaries are extrapolations, and there is no way of knowing how closely Thomas's expenses matched those of the "Victorian Web". But the budget as suggested gives a surplus of less than two shillings a week of income over expenditure, from which would have come such items as "club" money (i.e. sickness insurance) and luxuries such as tobacco. At any rate he could evidently manage, if only just, on his railway income while he was still employed. However, after his retirement in 1893 his income was severely reduced, and he can only have survived on savings made during his working life. He left no record of these, but there are indications in the diaries that he had got some funds in the bank that he could draw on from time to time. At one point he managed to make a loan to his signalman colleague Upton, and on another occasion he gave his daughter Sarah-Anne £5 to buy a sewing machine – something like a month's wages. Perhaps this was how he used his earnings from hoop making, putting them to one side for a rainy day and to supplement his superannuation payment of 6/6d a week. Of that there is no record, but we are left with the picture of a man who managed his finances very carefully and who supplemented his money income by self-sufficiency.

Five shillings in pre-decimal currency – half- a-crown (two shillings and sixpence), with a florin (two shillings) and a sixpenny piece.
In decimal currency 5/- would be 25p, which represented about a quarter of Thomas's weekly wages from the railway Company

CHAPTER 5

THE DIARIES

It is convenient to call these little books diaries, but they cover a wider range than the term suggests. As well as day-to-day entries with reports of events in the family or the village they comprise business accounts of Thomas's work in the woods and records of when he was on duty in the signal box. Scattered throughout the writings are gardening and other tips, bits of information from newspapers or elsewhere that caught his eye and copious observations, mostly of a religious nature, together with cuttings from the papers about whatever attracted his curiosity (which is to say a great deal).

There are three notebooks devoted entirely to records of the different areas of woodland his little gang worked in, when they were there, how many of each kind of hoops they cut and how much money they made from them. Sometimes there is an indication of whom the hoops were made for. This presumably means the dealer who bought them for onward sale to the coopers who made the barrels. Such names as William Marchant, Mr Godsmark and John Ireland crop up frequently. Sometimes "Uncle" is mentioned, who was no doubt that same John Ireland, the businessman of Kelsey House. The earliest systematic record is for the year 1845, although in what looks like a note added later Thomas also refers to work in earlier years as far back as 1835, when he was a boy of 11 years old. You started work young in those days.

These three account books give some insight into how Thomas and his little group worked but they also raise the odd question. Although some of their sites were local, occasionally the men went quite far afield for the coppiced woodlands where they made their hoops. In 1848 they were in Bletchingly, fifteen or twenty miles away to the north, and Sanderstead another four or five miles farther on. By then the London to Brighton railway was up and running and you could no doubt get to these places by train from Balcombe, but you would still have had to walk from, say, Merstham station, and the fares would have eaten into their profits. One wonders whether they did in fact commute from home or whether they stayed in lodgings near where they were working. Or perhaps they lived under canvas or in temporary hutted encampments, as the charcoal burners did, getting home from time to time to escape the winter cold. Thomas makes no

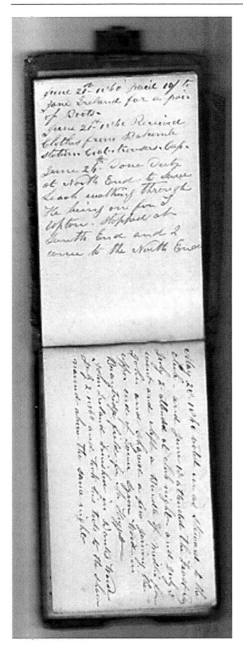

mention of any of this, and it is all a matter of conjecture. What is clear is that their profits were pretty meagre. In the 1847-48 season from about November to April they made around £133, but that was shared between Thomas, his father and his brothers George and James. The following season £126 had to be divided between six, as the previous four were joined by Thomas's other brothers John and Jonathan.

The earliest diary proper, that for 1860 and 1861, is a little pocket book bound in embossed leather. Its shape and size together with the wear on the cover suggest that Thomas may have carried it about with him in his waistcoat pocket. The miniature handwriting matches the small pages, of which some are in "portrait" format, allowing the writer to hold the book conveniently open in one hand rather than flat on a table. One imagines

Thomas penning his jottings as he spent free moments between trains standing in his signal box. This small book is something of a microcosm of all the others, containing in its small compass so many of the elements found throughout the diaries. The first few pages alone contain entries as varied as details of his signalman duty days and of his work in the woods, as well as information such as his being elected steward of The Club and the fact that he paid 10/- for a pair of boots and got his railway uniform. That was in June 1860. Entries continue in the same vein for a few months, but by November there is a page devoted only to a list of the different barrel hoops Thomas made in Flatfield Wood that month – fourteen foots, midlin, long and short pipe, hogshead, kilderkin, firkin, pink and bottle. Next there is a list (Thomas loved lists) of what he paid out on various outgoings, like rent, wood and coal. Soon it is back to daily notes about the January weather (*"Little on the give"*) and the fact that he broke his watch. The book is an eclectic mix of many varied aspects of Thomas's daily life, presenting a rich picture of what occupied him, even though it takes some patient reading to unravel the different threads.

We know nothing of Thomas's schooling beyond a diary entry for 12th November 1874, which records that

Old Mr Thomas Gibbs died this morning, near 83 years old. He used to be Clerk at the Church when I was a boy – and teach in the Sunday School....His wife kept the Day School and was my old School Mistress.

In the 1830's the day school was probably a so-called dame school. Such schools were often conducted in the home of the teacher, who was almost always a woman and often illiterate, so their standards were quite varied. Some provided no more than day care, while others gave a good foundation in the basics. A study conducted in 1838 by the Statistical Society of London found that nearly half of all pupils surveyed were only taught spelling, with a negligible number being taught mathematics and grammar. At any rate Mr and Mrs Gibbs seemed to be amongst the better teachers, evidently sparking off young Thomas's curiosity and imagination in a manner that remained with him throughout his life. His little books are pervaded with facts and ideas that he felt impelled to find out about, and then, of course, write down.

This entry in a booklet devoted entirely to notes, remarks and

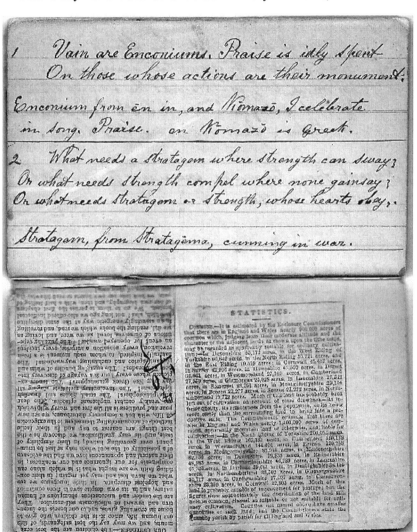

cuttings, is typical. Here Thomas teaches himself some classical Greek in order to explain to himself the exact meaning of the word "encomium" which he has encountered somewhere. The cutting from a newspaper is about agricultural history, discussing the progress of the enclosure of common land. Thomas had no personal interest in this matter but read about it to satisfy his curiosity concerning such an important development. There is unfortunately no indication of the date of this cutting, but it serves as an illustration of how his horizons were so much wider than his immediate surroundings. Self-education indeed.

The two pages below are from the back of the diary for 1884 (from a copy obtained from the West Sussex Record Office in Chichester). Here Thomas has set himself a number of mathematical problems. They are practical matters, such as finding the area of a triangle or the diameter of an iron rod of a given length whose volume is known. But they are set out as questions from a school textbook. Perhaps he found one of his children's books and wanted to be as well informed as they were, since they were the product of the educational reforms that led to the 1870 Education Act. Again, here is Thomas stretching his mind – mental exercise for its own sake.

The little books are in remarkably good condition for their age. Some have a little brass clasp to hold the covers closed when they were not in use so as to prevent the pages from getting dog-eared. Most look as if they had been kept safely in a drawer or on a shelf, to be taken down and brought up to date whenever their author had the time or inclination. Many have Thomas's name on the front, some with the added inscription "Diary for 18—". The earlier diaries were faithfully kept up day by day, if only with a brief comment on the weather or perhaps successive entries like "cleft some more", following a report of cleaving some coppiced rods at a particular site that required several days (probably rather monotonous) work. In later years the entries were more sporadic, maybe because Thomas was unwell and just didn't feel like writing up his books. The journal entries eventually faded out, but he never gave in. Shortly before he died he was still writing up his comments in the last of his notebooks.

Thomas clearly laid great store by these books. They were where he recorded almost everything that was important to him. About his family he recorded when his children were "short-clothed", that is when they graduated from baby clothes, or when they first went to school and how they progressed there (if they were doing well, at any rate). He wrote down when any of the family had new boots or when he bought himself a (New) Testament or had his watch mended. Improvements to his house were noted, as were particulars of when he paid his rent or bought coal for the fire. The text that the preacher used Sunday by Sunday in the little chapel was faithfully set down. His working schedule in the signal box as well as details of where he worked in the woods and precisely how many of each kind of hoop he produced – all was carefully noted down. We can see justification for recording particulars of his work as a hoopmaker, but we have to wonder what was the point of this relentless setting down of detail. What did he actually do with all this information? The answer is probably very little. The point lay not in the reading of the notes once written down but in the writing of them in the first place. This methodical man simply loved facts and he loved ordering them. His diaries were the expression of his orderly mind.°

CHAPTER 6

THE PARCEL RE-WRAPPED

A untie Win's brown paper parcel had contained seventeen of her
grandfather's diaries, three account books and three note books
of extracts from a variety of sources together with a number of
newspaper cuttings. And there was the 1884 diary that mysteriously
appeared in the West Sussex Record Office. The collection doesn't
always make up a straightforward narrative and the diaries don't
necessarily make easy reading. But then we shouldn't expect them to.
After all they represent Thomas's daily life with all its disparate
elements, and which one of any of us leads a life that can be neatly
compartmentalised and related as a coherent story.

And yet, taken as a whole, they give a remarkable picture of how
this man lived his life. They show how hard he worked, and how he
managed to balance his work in the woods with his duties in the
signal box. They set out how he organised and tabulated his hoop
making business, giving us what is possibly unique insight into the
way this trade worked. They show how he kept a check on when he
was on signalman duty. They indicate how he kept his personal
financial affairs in order to his own satisfaction, too, although it is
difficult to follow the exact sequence. They show Thomas's deep
piety and his love of reading, mostly it appears of works of an
"improving" nature – he was a true Victorian. There are many
recollections of his father, who died two years before the first diary
entry, and plenty of references to his mother, to whom he seems to
have been very close. The doings of his wife Ellen and even more of

his six surviving children appear frequently. Thomas's eldest child, Sarah-Ann, later Aunt Annie, the mother of Auntie Win, seems to have been a particular favourite. So the diaries show him as a devoted family man. He often recorded natural events, such as the dates on which he first heard the cuckoo or the nightingale or witnessed a meteor (7th September, 1868, 11.50.pm *It lighted the box up like a blaze notwithstanding the lamps and Firelight*). He was an observer of the local scene, recording events in the village and significant developments on the railway, like the re-laying of the permanent way, and the installation of a telegraph to link the two ends of the tunnel, a preliminary to the evolution of modern signalling.

Through the diaries, then, we can get to know the man. They show a countryman who was far from a simple rustic. Hoop making may have been a traditional rural craft, but Thomas brought sophistication to the way he organised it. And in joining the railway company he made a quantum leap into the developing industrial world. Here was a capable man who was on top of his job – or jobs. He spent his whole life in a small Sussex village, but in today's world he could certainly have coped with a managerial post, whether in the railway industry or elsewhere. Or he might have brought his knowledge to bear in modern forestry, say, or in running a bespoke furniture making company.

So Thomas reveals himself through his diaries. And yet there are questions that remain tantalisingly unanswered. For instance, how was it that Thomas came to be associated with Providence Chapel. Did he go there out of curiosity or out of dissatisfaction with the parish church of St Mary's? And why did he apparently stop going there in 1874? Was it because of the "much trouble" or for some other reason? Why was he so bitter towards the Roman Catholic Church? Did his attitude come about before he started going to the chapel or was it a result of his attendance? Balcombe was hardly a papist stronghold and quite possibly he never actually discussed these matters with any Roman Catholics at all. Why then was he so vociferous in his condemnation of them?

Perhaps a more fundamental question is why Thomas wrote a diary at all. Some reasons are obvious, like the need to keep records of his workings in the woods and of the cash transactions that followed. And it was natural to set down when he was on duty and when and by whom he was relieved. Family events were recorded, such as the birth of his children (*Ellen confined of a son*) or simply of visits to or from relatives.

For Thomas to write about all this is quite understandable. But why did he record such minute detail about his everyday life as for example when he had his boots or his watch repaired and how much it cost? Why did he find it necessary to report on the weather for several days in succession and then not to comment on it at all for months at a time? What was the point of writing down long lists of sometimes unconnected happenings apparently copied out from the newspaper? Sometimes it looks as if he didn't keep his diary to rely on it as a record, but just as a kind of hobby, simply enjoying the pleasure that writing it gave him.

There is another perspective, too. At times it is as if he were writing journalistically for someone else to read. He supplies explanations that seem to be directed towards the external reader, since he wouldn't need them himself. So for example he refers to Kelsey House that was Uncle John's, where one would have expected him to remember that his uncle had lived there without having to remind himself. And when on 12th November 1874 old Mr Gibbs died, why did Thomas write down that the old man had taught in the Sunday School and that his wife had been Thomas's school mistress, since he clearly remembered these facts perfectly well anyway in order to be able to write them down? Was he perhaps subconsciously writing for posterity? Could there have been the thought there somewhere that a century and a half in the future someone might pick up his diaries and be intrigued by what he wrote?

We can never know what lay at the back of Thomas's mind. Let us just be thankful that this remarkable man did write so much down and reveal so much of himself in the process. And let us be equally thankful that people such as Auntie Win preserved it all.

Thomas and Ellen Ireland in about 1890

APPENDIX 1

NOTES, CUTTINGS, REMEDIES AND TIPS

Thomas loved facts, especially ones about extraordinary phenomena and occurrences, which he must have gathered from reading. He had a habit of writing them down in his diaries, sometimes in the pages left at the end of a year, sometimes in odd spaces throughout the books.

They can be considered under various categories, of which a large one is simply lists of events or anniversaries. There are far too many of these to quote in full, but by way of example, a note in the 1867 diary records that:-

> *The largest Salmon ever taken within the memory of man on a British River by rod and fly, was taken in the Tweed, about Novbr 1867 – it turned the scales after being freely bled at 51 lbs.*

And that:-

> *The iron framework of the Paris Exhibition weighed 27000000 lbs, in the whole there were 6000000 rivets, for the plating of which 15000000 holes had to be punched.*

The same notebook contains a sort of home-made encyclopædia, nearly 100 facts about historical and other personages arranged in alphabetical order and set down in Thomas's careful hand. So we can learn that Columbus was born at Coconato, Piedmont, that one Henry Jenkins died in 1670, aged 169, and that Ulysses was King of Theaki, the ancient Ithaca, an Ionian island.

Often groups of entries concerning a particular topic seem to have been made at the same time, filling up the spare pages in the notebook at the end of a year's diary. So at the end of the 1873 diary for instance a couple of pages are devoted to commemorating the deaths of naval veterans:–

In Febr. 1873 an Old Trafalgar Veteran died aged 94.

Like most of the note-books this diary contains tantalising and eclectic jottings whose significance for the writer can only be guessed at.

Man carries his superiority inside, animals theirs outside.
*The Crab Fish and the Chelifer (*sic*) insect walk sideways.*

There is even a little joke:-

Captain BBBB sent His CCCC to the De Da Ds Dt for Potatoes,
with a somewhat ponderous explanation:
Captain Fourbees sent His Forces to the East Indies for Potatoes. East is in the four D's.

Other jottings fall into five main groups: food recipes, gardening, remedies for various ailments, religious observations and sundry tips. The religious notes take up a large portion of the little books, but apart from those dealt with in Chapter 3 *"Church and Chapel"* it is very difficult to categorise them, and it is frankly hard to share Thomas's enthusiasm for them. The recipes and remedies are more accessible, but in some cases the quantities and the nature of the ingredients may seem odd to modern eyes. We should remind ourselves that the circumstances of Thomas's life were very different from those of our own day. The kitchen garden was his supermarket. He had a large family to feed and support, so he had to be largely self-supporting in food and other commodities, and this is reflected in the amount of food and the way he produced it. Moreover the technological perceptions of his day were often very different from those of today. We should certainly not assume for instance that a remedy for "the itch", which includes quicksilver or mercury is safe or appropriate for our own use. However, they are set down here exactly as Thomas wrote them down. They make a long list (so perhaps in this they reflect Thomas's own proclivity), but they are included in order to give an impression of some of the ways this Victorian dealt with the minutiae of life.

FOOD RECIPES

Baking powder (near the end of 1895 diary) –

To make Baking Powder.
¼ lb   Carbonate Soda
2 oz   Tartaric Acid
½   Corn Flower
½   ground Rice

Ice Cream (Near the end of 1868 diary) –

Lemon Ice Cream.
Take one pint of cream, rasp two lemons on sugar, squeeze them, and add the juice with ½ lb of sugar; mix; freeze.

Ginger Ice Cream.
Bruise 6 oz the very best preserved ginger in a mortar; add the juice of one Lemon, ½ lb sugar, one pint of cream; mix well; strain through a hair sieve; freeze.

Muffins (1874 diary, end of September)

Muffins to make.

Flour 1 quartern [i.e ¼ pint] *warm milk and water 1½ pint, yeast ¼ pint, salt 2 oz, mix for 15 minutes, then add ¼ peck* [i.e. 4 pints] *of flour, make a dough, let it rise 1 hour, roll it up, pull it in pieces, make into balls, put it in a warm place. Shape into muffins, and bake in tins, turn when half done, dip into warm milk and bake to a pale brown.*

Toffee (End of 1866 diary)

To make toffee, put into a saucepan ½ lb of Brown Sugar, ¼ lb of Butter and a little Essence of Lemon or peppermint. Let it simmer over a slow fire very gently untill it obtains such a consistency that an iron skewer will stand in it. Add a few Blanched almonds before it is quite cold.

Yeast (End of 1868 diary, ⅓ through the book)

Patent Yeast. Boil 6 oz of Hops in 3 gallons of water 3 hours; strain it off and let it stand 10 minutes; then add half a Peck [i.e. 1 gallon] *of ground Malt, stir well up, and cover it over; return the hops, and put the same quantity of water to them again, boiling them as before, straining it off to the first Mash; stir it up, and let it remain 4 hours, then strain it off, and set it to work at 90 degrees, with 3 pints of patent yeast; let it stand about 24 hours; take the scum off the top and strain it through a Hair Sieve, it will then be fit for use; one pint is sufficient to make a Bushel* [i.e. 8 gallons] *of Bread.*

GARDENING TIPS

Celery (Notebook "N 1838" December)

Celery – Keep the earth from running into the heart of the plant. Do not press the earth to closely at the upper part of the plant, tie each plant loosely removing the succors [sic]

and small leaves, then add a little earth every week. Let it
get a good size then earth it up adding a little water often.

Celery cultivation (1867 diary, ⅔ through)

There is no mystery in growing Celery. Dig a trench one
foot wide and one foot deep; fork up the bottom and put 3
inches thick of dung all over it, and stir it among its own
thickness of the earth. Dibble in your plants 9 inches apart
along the middle of the bottom, and water them well in; as
they grow you draw the earth to them, and when the trench
is full you bank up to them.

Celery (Near end of 1867 diary)

Incomparable Dwarf White is the best Family Celery

Cabbage (1890 diary, January)

Ellams Early Dwarf Spring Cabbage may be sown about the
10th of July for early spring cutting.

Dung (End of 1868 diary)

Poultry dung is very strong; a ¼ of a peck [i.e ½ gallon]
should be dissolved in 10 gallons of water, and then should
only be used for one watering in four.

Dung (End of 1869 diary)

The dung of all animals that live on vegetables is good for
Land. Those which live on flesh give it strong enough to
poison. Sheep, Cow, Rabbit, Deer, Horse may be used with
safety. Poultry must be mixed with 10 times its weight of
sand, peat or common earth, to bring it down to the
standard of other fertilisers; it matters little how it is
applied. Top dressing is good in wet weather.

Grafting Wax (1868 diary, towards the end)

Resin and beeswax make grafting wax, but it must be
tempered with tallow grease, so that it may be laid on

merely warm and harden when cold.

Pears (1868 diary, towards the end)
Bon chretien Pear grows in France.

Seed testing (Near end of 1867 diary)
Seeds, to test the quality of, put some in water and expose them to a gentle heat for 24 Hours, the good seed alone will sprout. Or immerse thoroughly in water, when the dead and non-productive will swim, and the sound will sink.

Seed Quantities (1868 diary, end)

Seeds required to Sow Kitchen Garden Plots.	
Asparagus bed, 15 sq yds.	*½ Pint*
Beans, Broad, row 3 ft	*1 Quart*
Beans, Kidney, do.	*½ Pint*
Beet, row 50 ft	*1 oz*
Brocoli, 4 sq. yds.	*½ oz*
Brussels Sprouts, 4 sq. yds.	*½ oz*
Cabbage, bed 3 sq.yds.	*½ oz*
Carrots, drill of 120 ft.	*1 oz*
Cauliflower, 4 sq. yds.	*½ oz*
Celery, 4 sq. yds.	*½ oz*
Cress, 3 sq. yds.	*1 oz*
Endive, 4 sq. yds.	*½ oz*
Kale, 4 sq. yds.	*½ oz*
Leek, 2 sq. yds.	*½ oz*
Lettuce, 4 sq. yds.	*½ oz*
Mushroom, 7 sq. yds.	*1 Bushel* [= 8 gallons]
Onions, 9 sq. yds.	*1 oz*
Parsley, row 8 feet	*1 oz*
Parsnip, drill of 200 ft.	*1 oz*
Peas, early, row 60 ft.	*1 pint*
Pease, Large, late, row 30 ft.	*1 Pint*
Potatoes, row 30 ft.	*½Peck* [= 1 gallon]
Radishes, 4 sq. yds.	*1 oz*

Savoy, do.	½ oz
Spinach, drill of 120 ft.	1 oz
Turnip, 4 sq. yds.	½ oz

The Scarlet invincible Pea is quite as hardy as the rest.

Sowing (End of 1868 diary)

Sow. The Figures denote in which week of the month to sow.

Jan	Fe	Ma	Ap	Ma	Ju	Jul	Au	Nov	
	2	2					2	2	Peas, Early
		2	2	2	2	2			" Late
	3	2							Potatoes, Early
		2							" Late
2	2	2	2	2	2	2	2	2	Radish, Turnip
		1							Rhubarb
		2	2						Savoy
		1							Sea Kale
	2	2	2	2	2	2	1		Spinach
	2	2	2	2	2	2	1		Turnip
			2	1					Vegetable Marrow
		2	2	2					Pot herbs

Sow. The Figures denote in which week of the month to sow.

Jan	Fe	Ma	Ap	Ma	Ju	Jul	Au	Sep	
	3	2	2	2			2		Carrot, Early
		1							" Late
	2	3							Celery
	2				1				Corn Salad
2	2	2	2	2	2	2	2		Cress and Mustard
			4	2					Cucumber
			3	2					Gourd
			3	2					Kohl Rabi
	2	2							Leek
	2	2	2	2	2	2	1		Lettuce
	2						3	2	Onions
	1								Parsnips
	1	1	2						Parsley

Sow. The Figures denote in which week of the month to sow.

Jan	Fe	Ma	Ap	Ma	Ju	Jul	Au	Sep	
		2							Asparagus
2	2				2	2			Beans, Broad
	2	2	2	2	2				" Windsor
		3	2	2	1				" French Dwarf
		3	2						" Scarlet Runner
				1					Beet
	1	2							Borecol,* and Kale
	1	2	1						Brocoli, Early
	2	2							" Late
	2	2							Brussel Sprouts
	1	2		2					Cabbage, Early
		1	3	2					" for Colewarts*
2	2						3	2	Cauliflower, Early
	2	2	2	2					" Late

[*Borecole and Colewarts – unknown. Presumably some kind of cabbage]

Vegetables (Back of 1868 diary)

Best Vegetables for a Small Garden
Scarlet-blossomed broad bean, Becks green gem bean,
Negro french bean, Common scarlet runner bean, Short
horn carrot, Tom Thumb, Suttons early coombe, and
rosette cabbage; Australian cress; Tom thumb and
London cos lettuce, Silver skin onion, Double curled
parsley, Bishops long pod, Princess royal, Advancer and
Veitches perfection peas; Custard vegetable marrow, Golden
globe, Rivers royal ashleaf, and Prince of Wales Kidney
Potatoes. These are selected generally because of their
compact habit of growth and general usefulness.
Cauliflower is a summer vegetable. Brocoli is more a
winter production.
Any good early potato may be taken up in June quite ripe,
and if planted again may be dug in November as new
potatoes, or covered from frost, may be dug as wanted
till spring.

Vines (1868 diary, near the end)

Vines in proper soil, do not require periodical manuring. There are many ways of pruning the Vine: where you confine the growth to one rod up each rafter you may prune all the side shoots very close, even to a single eye. The Vines in France generally blossom about the beginning of June. This year 1868 they were in blossom the 29th May.

Vines (1867 diary, ¾ through)

Remove Vines after the fall of the leaf, and before the swelling of the buds

Various (End of 1867 diary, in middle of book)

Peas, a pint should sow 60 feet of Row –
Beans, a pint should sow 80 feet of Row –
Kidney beans will do 169 feet –
The Cabbage tribe, an oz should sow 8 sq yards –
Carrots, an oz will sow 150 feet of drills –
Onions, an oz will cover 9 sq yards –
Parsley, an oz will sow 150 feet of drills or edging –
Beetroot, an oz will do 150 feet of drills –
Turnip, Half an oz will sow 10 sq yards –
As to the distance of drills, Peas should be as far apart as the peas grow tall, 3 feet peas 3 feet apart, etc. Carrots should be 6 to 8 inches. runners 6 feet. French Beans 2 feet. Parsley if in drills 18 inches. Dwarf Beans 2 feet.

REMEDIES

Beverage (Inside front cover of 1863 diary)

Good Beverage. Decoctions of demulcent herbs, such as Colts Foot, Harehound or particularly marshmallow roots and Iceland moss. Sweetened with a small quantity of Sugar Candy.

Consumption (Back of 1862 diary)

For Consumption
Take one pound of Loaf Sugar. Dissolve in half a pint of
cold water in a clean saucepan. Take the Syrup off the fire
before it quite boils; when cold add to this quantity 1oz of
tincture of tolu and shake well.

Cough (Inside front cover of 1863 diary)

For a cough
1 oz Syrup of Marshmallow
1 oz Syrup of White Poppies
1 oz Oxymell Squills
1 oz Oil Sweet Almonds
1 oz Sarregaric [?] Elixer
Shake it and take a tea spoonful 2 or 3 times a day.

Eye lotion (Near end of 1867 diary)

Eye Lotion, Acetate of Zink, ½ a drachm [i.e 1/16 oz];
Distilled water 16 oz. Mix it.

Ears (End of 1861 diary)

For pains in the Ears. Drop a little oil of sweet almonds in
the Ear.

"Itch" (Beginning of 1862 diary)

6 pennyworth of Quicksilver, 2 do of Cypatty [?] powder,
¼ lb of Hogs Lard. Simmer it all together and stir it till it is
thick. This is for the itch.

Hoarseness (End of 1861 diary)

For Hoarseness. Take of sugar and rectified spirit of wine
so as just to wet it and take it 3 or 4 nights going to bed – if
the body be feverish use a little salad oil with the above.

Liver (End of 1861 diary)

For the Liver. The liver of a Hare dried and beaten into a powder is good for all the diseases of the liver of man.

Pimples (End of 1861 diary)

For a face full of red pimples. Dissolve camphire [or camphor?] in vinegar and mix it with celandine water and wash the face with it.

Quinsy (End of 1861 diary)

For the Quinsey. Bleeding is good. It were very convenient that a syrup and an ointment of orpine were always ready to drink the one and anoint the throat with the other.

Scurf (Beginning of 1862 diary)

Scurf on the face. Use clarified honey after washing and let it remain on.

Sprain (End of 1861 diary)

An ointment for a new sprain. Take of the Rozin of the pine tree, of the purest turpentine, yellow wax washed, pure oil – of each equal parts. Melt them into an ointment.

Toothache (End of 1861 diary)

For the toothache. Take the inner rind of and [sic] Elder tree and bruise it and put thereto a little pepper and make it into balls and hold them between the teeth that ache.

Voice loss (1869 diary, end of August)

When the voice is lost from the effects of Cold, beat the white of egg, and mix with the juice of one Lemon, and white sugar.

Whooping cough (Start of 1862 diary)

For the Whooping Cough. Mercury with Chalk 3 grains [i.e.1/146 oz], Sulphate of Potash 6 grains [i.e. 1/73 oz], powdered Rhubarb 6 grains. For Children under 5 years ⅔ of the quantity, and under 1 year divide it into two doses.

Wounds and ulcers (End of 1861 diary)

To cleanse wounds and ulcers. Take of the juice of Smallage [?] one pound, honey 9 ounces, wheat flour three ounces. Boil them to a just thickness.

OTHER TIPS

Adhesive (Inside back cover of 1862 diary)

Adhesive Composition. Glue and water with a small mixture of sweet oil; a little treacle or sugar prevents the curling up or twisting.

Bait (Notebook "N1868", page 108)

The Bait for Roach should be gentles, red paste, boiled wheat or malt. The ground bait should be boiled malt or bran mixed with clay, in which are a few dead gentles. In fishing for Roach in ponds, chew and throw in white bread, baiting with a large gentle.

Book preservation (1862 diary, inside front cover)

To preserve Books – a few drops of any perfumed oil will preserve from mould and damp.

Bullfinches

Best food for the young Bullfinch is is crumbs of bread baked in Boiling milk with an equal quantity of bruised and soaked Rape seed; as they grow up poppy and millet seed, sprouting corn, lettuce and water cresses, fruit and nuts should be given them. When full grown they may have Fir and pine seeds, most berries that have kernels, buds of the Beech, maple, oak and other trees, Seeds of the nettle and cruciform plant. When unwell give them steeped rape seed and change them about, and when moulting put a rusty nail in the water, and give them nourishing food and a few ants Eggs.

Dyeing

Dyeing: Cochineal for red, saffron for yellow. Ronas a root dies a beautiful red. Brazil, a wood brought from Brazil is of great use in dyeing red.

Etching

Etching upon Egg Shells – Cover the shells with appropriate Designs in tallow or varnish and immerse in strong acetic acid. They will then come out in strong relief.

Fire lighting (1869 diary, end of December)

On a damp day before lighting the fire, after it is laid, light a piece of paper or shavings on the top – it will prevent gas or smoke.

Game ("N 1868" page 108)

Game is in season during the following portions of the year. Grouse 12th of August to 10th December. Partridges 1st September to 1st February. Bustards 1st September to 1st March. Pheasants 1st October to 1st February.

Grease Stains

To remove Grease Stains from Cloth; Moisten the stains with a few drops of concentrated solution of Sub-carbonate of potash; rub the part between the fingers, and then wash the cloth with a little warm water.

Honey Soap (Notebook "N 1838" November-December)

To make Honey Soap. Cut 2 lbs of yellow soap thin in a double saucepan, stirring till melted. Put the soap in the inner one and water in outer one, then add ¼ lb of palm oil, ¼ lb of Honey, 3 pennyworth of true oil of cinnamon. Let it boil together 6 or 8 minutes, pour it out and stand it till next day; it is then fit to use.

Ink (Inside cover of 1962 diary)

Blue ink – two drachms [i.e.¼ fluid ounce] *oxalic acid, two ditto prussian blue, to be mixed in ½ pint of water.*

Green ink. Dissolve six drachms of the crystals of virdigris in a pint of distilled water and add five drachms [i.e. 5/8 fluid ounce] *of gum arabic and two drachms* [i.e. 1/4 ounce] *of white sugar. A fine green ink may be made with a strong decoction of elm bark to which green vitriol* [i.e. copper sulphate] *is added when cold.*

Mahogany stain (Beginning of 1862 diary)

Mahogany artificial. Plane the surface smooth, then rub with a solution of nitrous acid. Then mix one oz. of dragons blood [a red gum that exudes from the fruit of some palms and the dragon tree] *in nearly a pint of spirits of wine to dissolve and ⅓ of an oz. Of carbonate of soda mixed together, then put it on with a soft brush and repeat it at short intervals.*

To remove stains from the hands damp them with water then rub them with tartaric acid or salt of Lemons as you would soap, then rinse them and wipe them dry – one third of the salt of Lemon or the acid with water put to stains on linen or muslin and laid in the sun and wet once or twice with cold water will remove the stains.

Pencil mark preservation (Beginning of 1862 diary)

Pencil marks to preserve. Dip the paper into a decoction of skim milk then dry it and iron it on the wrong side; do not let the iron stand on it but move quick.

Stain (Inside back cover of 1862 diary)

To stain musical instruments.
Crimson. Boil one pound of ground Brazil wood in 3 quarts of water for an hour. Strain it and add ½ oz. of cochineal. Boil it again for ½ an hour gently – it will be then fit for

use.
Purple. Boil a pound of chip Log wood in 3 quarts of water for an hour then add 4 oz. of alum.

Incomparable White Dwarf Celery

THE FAMILY NAME

The origin of the surname Ireland is a little obscure. The name is not particularly widespread nationally, although there are local areas of the country where it is not uncommon. Around Liverpool, for example, the name crops up frequently. Presumably this is because movement between the island of Ireland and the British mainland focused on Liverpool and Irish people who settled round there were identified by their origin. But the English have always been notoriously vague about those they regard as foreigners, and for many in the Anglo-Saxon heartland of the south and east the terms "Irish" and "Scotch" were more or less interchangeable, denoting simply people who came from somewhere out there to the British north or west. So the name Ireland may not necessarily indicate someone who came originally from across the Irish Sea but just an incomer from somewhere else in the British Isles.

At any rate the name is found in Sussex and Surrey, and there is no evidence here to suggest any connection with the Emerald Isle or anywhere else. Thomas's ancestors can be traced back to the Surrey town of Dorking where George and Jane Ireland lived in the early years of the 18th century. There are other bearers of the name thereabouts, including some with the spelling Ierland, who can be dated in the 17th century, but although they may be related no positive link can be found. George and Jane's third child John, born in nearby Newdigate in 1747, married Sarah Penfold, herself a native of Dorking. At some point this couple evidently moved for some reason to the Sussex village of Balcombe, twenty miles or so away, and so made the first link with the village where Irelands lived for the next two hundred years. Eventually they were both buried in the churchyard there. At the time of their marriage in 1775 neither could read or write, but they had a long life together, for Sarah died at the age of 82 and John was 85. To judge from the scale of their gravestone[1] with its long inscription their relatives held them in high enough regard to want to remember them in this way. Their first surviving child, (born 1778) was also called John. This John eventually became a successful local wood merchant, a member of the businessmen's club in Horley and died a rich man with an estate of £3000. Perhaps it was he whose wealth provided the gravestone for his parents (although his sister Becky is described in one record as "a pauper").

John senior was probably a woodland worker, a maker of barrel hoops, perhaps. Although his entrepreneurial son John took his career beyond this, his other sons, George, Thomas and James, would have spent their lives working alongside their father as a small gang in the woods within three or four miles of their native village. Thomas, the third son, was born on 25th February, 1781. At the age of 37 he married Anne Botting (or Botten). She was born on 13th April 1797 in the Black Dog Inn, a medieval building that still stands as a private house just behind the shops in Crawley High Street. Their marriage took place in the lovely old Saxon church at Worth, a couple of miles away, and they settled in Balcombe, probably in a cottage known as the Alley House, just behind the village forge opposite the "Half Moon" inn and Balcombe Store. They had five sons, of whom the firstborn, on 14th December 1824, was Thomas, our diarist, signalman and hoopmaker. By and by this Thomas married Ellen of Horsham, daughter of Simeon and Mary Stenning. Their seven children included Sarah-Ann, born 1863, mother of Auntie Win; George, born 1865, father of Frank and my grandfather, and John ("Uncle Jack"), born 1875, sometime manager of Balcombe waterworks.

---

1 F17 on churchyard plan

So there were members of the Ireland family in Balcombe for at least five generations. The last to carry the name in Balcombe was Rupert, a great-nephew of Thomas, who died in the early 1990's. The most recent known descendants of the Balcombe Irelands are Thomas's great-great-great-grandchildren, Joshua, born 2001, and Alice, born 2003, children of my son David; and Stan, born 2006 and Kate, born 2008, children of my daughter Helen.

Pedigree of the Irelands

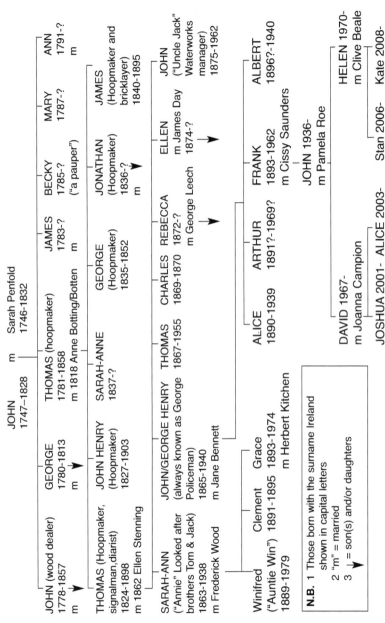

N.B. 1 Those born with the surname Ireland
shown in capital letters

2 "m" = married

3 ↓ = son(s) and/or daughters

APPENDIX 3

St Mary's. Balcombe. Sx.

Scale: metres.

THANK YOU

The whole point of this little book has been to let my great-grandfather Thomas Ireland speak for himself through his remarkable diaries. But sometimes he has needed a little help to make his meaning clear, and certainly I have needed support to explain the context in which he lived and worked. It has all taken time, I'm afraid, and some of the people to whom I owe thanks for their help are sadly no longer with us. To all those who have contributed information and advice I am extremely grateful.

Professor E.J.T. Collins, sometime Director of the Institute of Agricultural History at the University of Reading, provided the key explanation of the names of the various lengths of barrel hoop used by Thomas (midlin, bottle, long and short pipe, long and short pink, and so on). This led to an introduction to and understanding of the trade of the barrel hoop makers. Chapter 3 draws extensively on conversations and correspondence with Dr Collins and from his own contribution to Vol VI of *The Agrarian History of England and Wales 1750-1850*.

Leslie Fairweather's *Balcombe, the story of a Sussex village* was and remains a delight and a valuable source of facts and ideas.

The diaries of George Greenfield, Estate Carpenter and Clerk of the Works at Balcombe Place provided colourful insight into the life of the village in the 1870's and 1880's.

Mr D.H. Turner of Mill Lane, Balcombe, cast valuable light on the locations of the woodland sites named by Thomas. Although they have not been greatly used directly in the text they gave a most helpful picture of where he worked.

I am grateful to the County Record Offices of Surrey and East and West Sussex, and especially to the last-named for sending me photocopies of Thomas's diary for 1884 (Add MSS 49826, included here by permission of the County Archivist) and of the plan of Balcombe churchyard, originally drawn by Mrs Jean Shelley and reproduced here by the kind agreement of her son, Mr John Shelley.

The late Dr Kenneth Dix of the Strict Baptist Historical Society was very helpful in revealing the story of Providence Chapel and in suggesting his probable relationship with it.

The National Archives at Kew (formerly the Public Record Office) explained Thomas's employment on the railway.

I have drawn on various web-sites, notably those of www.ancestry.com for information about Thomas's family and background, www.victorianweb.org for his suggested budget, and www.spartacus.schoolnet.co.uk for information about the early history of the London to Brighton railway.

Many of the pictures are from my own photographs. The picture postcards of Balcombe viaduct and the tunnel entrance in Chapter 2, of the charcoal burners in Chapter 3, of St Mary's Church and of Providence Chapel in Chapter 4 do not carry the publisher's name and I have been unable to find one. The picture of a hoop-maker in Chapter 2 was given to me many years ago and I am afraid I cannot trace their origin.

My thanks go to Zoë Abbitt for checking the typescript and making a number of valuable suggestions.

My wife and family have been a source of advice and encouragement. Auntie Win gave me the diaries in the first place, and conversations with her in the subsequent year or two before she died in 1989 gave real colour to my understanding of her grandfather.

I have tried to trace appropriate copyright owners and offer my apologies to any whom I have omitted and ask them please to contact me. I sincerely thank all those on whose help I have relied, and I hope to have been true to them, but responsibility for any errors of fact or interpretation of course lies with me.

I am grateful for the advice and practical help of Dick Richardson of Country Books, without whom this book would not have come to publication.

JFI Autumn 2012

THE BOOK CLUB
FOR THOSE
WHO LOVE SUSSEX

So many books are written about Sussex that it's difficult to keep track of them all. Which is why, some twelve years ago, writer/publisher David Arscott launched his successful **Sussex Book Club** to keep enthusiasts abreast of everything that's being written about the county. Judy Moore took over from David in Spring 2011, and Dick Richardson of Country Books took the reins in Spring 2012.

Membership is completely free
You won't be sent books you haven't ordered
Books are sent free of post and packing charges

Two newsletters are sent to members – Spring/Summer and Autumn/Winter reviewing new books on Sussex. Those with access to email can opt for the A4 colour magazine. Books can be ordered and paid for on-line through PayPal on our website.

Contact the Sussex Book Club:
info@sussexbooks.co.uk

or visit the website:
www.sussexbooks.co.uk